CONTENTS

FOREWORD

In compiling this *A TUNE A DAY* course of tuition, the object has intentionally been not to cover too much ground, but to concentrate on the acquisition of a thorough, musical background and a solid technical foundation when studying the Classical Guitar.

The initial skills have been broken down into component parts and presented in a logical manner which, at the same time, allows the teacher wide latitude for expression of his individual views on guitar instruction. Introduction of the elements of notation has purposely been deferred until such knowledge is essential for further study (*p. 7*).

Close attention has been given to the development of the right-hand thumb and fingers confined to the open strings. With this *"One thing at a time"* preparation of the right-hand fingers, correlating the fingers of the left-hand becomes a simpler learning process. Each new feature is introduced ONLY when its employment is necessary to the progressive layout of the *A TUNE A DAY* grading. Fresh objectives are reached through a step-by-step presentation of the technique and musical data required for the immediate task in hand. This natural progression, which is characteristic of the *A TUNE A DAY* instruction books, will ensure a sound comprehension and systematic advancement on the basis of an expanding musicianship.

The student should be more concerned with the quality of his playing, than its quantitative aspect. Tonal dynamics when plucking the strings, correct note values, demand acute observance. The casual approach to nuance must be avoided and musical sensitivity fostered from the first stroke on the open strings.

ABOUT THE GUITAR

The designation "Classical" Guitar is a misnomer as it is no more classic than any other instrument. "Classical" refers to the style used in playing and has no reference to the type of music to be performed. Like the Piano the Classical Guitar is a complete instrument, being both melodic and harmonic. A better name might be "Finger Style Guitar", as compared with the "Plectrum (pick) Guitar".

The construction of the Classical Guitar and type of strings used, make it highly preferable where a varied quality of tone-colours and sustained harmonies are desirable.

A FEW POINTS TO REMEMBER

a Your progress is dependent upon the amount of carefully thought-out practice.
b Cultivate the habit of careful listening.
c Learn to analyse problems for yourself.
d The mastery of each new problem will enhance your interest.

Illustrations posed by Stanley George Urwin

THE GUITAR AND ITS COMPONENT PARTS

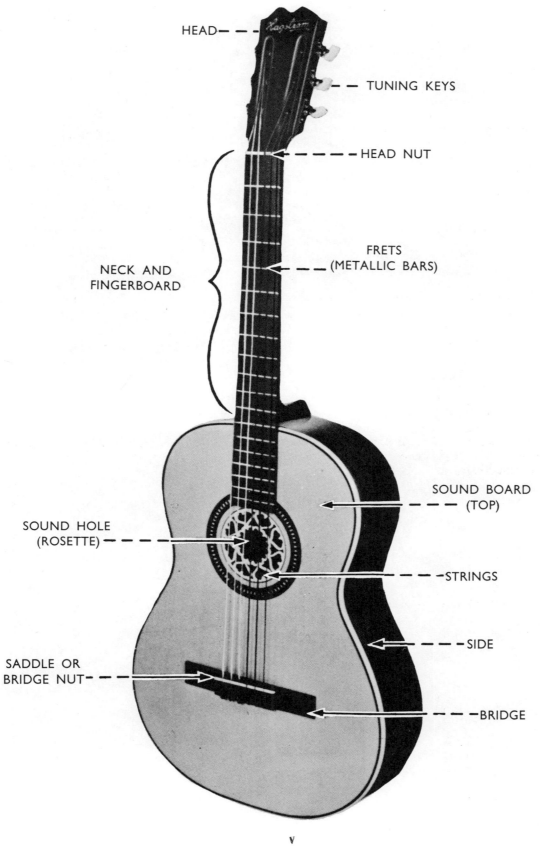

HEAD

TUNING KEYS

HEAD NUT

FRETS
(METALLIC BARS)

NECK AND
FINGERBOARD

SOUND BOARD
(TOP)

SOUND HOLE
(ROSETTE)

STRINGS

SIDE

SADDLE OR
BRIDGE NUT

BRIDGE

HOLDING THE GUITAR - PLAYING POSITION

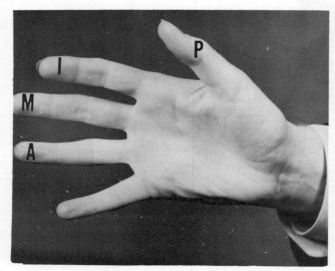

RIGHT HAND FINGERS

CROSS LEFT LEG OVER THE RIGHT KNEE

LEFT FOOT ON LOW STOOL

RIGHT HAND POSITION FOR PLUCKING THE STRINGS

LEFT HAND POSITIONS

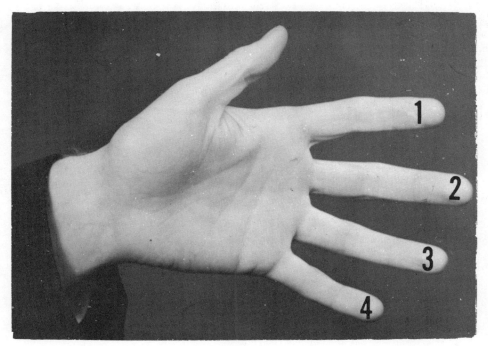

LEFT HAND FINGERS

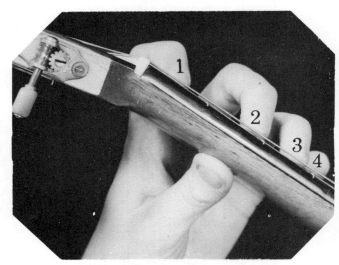

CORRECT LEFT THUMB POSITION

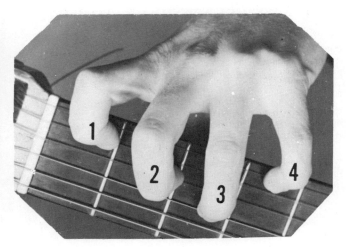

CORRECT PLACEMENT OF LEFT HAND FINGERS

TUNING THE GUITAR

Piano keyboard

FROM THE PIANO

The six open strings of the guitar should be tuned to the same pitch as the notes shown on the piano keyboard. Note that middle (C) is just to the left of the keyhole.

THE ACTUAL PITCH OF THE GUITAR IS ONE OCTAVE LOWER THAN THE WRITTEN NOTES ON THE STAVE.

THE GUITAR PITCH PIPE

Pitch pipes giving the correct pitch of the six open strings are obtainable from music stores. WHEN TUNING FROM A PITCH PIPE BE SURE THE STRINGS ARE PITCHED ONE OCTAVE *LOWER* THAN THAT SOUNDING ON THE PIPE.

TUNING WITHOUT PIANO OR PITCH PIPE

As the lowest string (E) will vary the least in pitch we might use this string as a starting point and tune the other strings as follows (see Fig. 1):

Place finger just behind the 5th fret of the low (E) 6th string, and tune the 5th string to the same pitch. (A)
　Stop the (A) string at the 5th fret and tune the 4th string to the same pitch. (D)
　Stop the (D) string at the 5th fret and tune the 3rd string to the same pitch. (G)
　Stop the (G) string at the FOURTH fret and tune the 2nd string to the same pitch. (B)
　Stop the (B) string at the 5th fret and tune the 1st string to the same pitch. (E)

written for the piano actual pitch

E A D G B E

written for the guitar sounds one octave lower

E A D G B E

E-6　A-5　D-4　G-3　B-2　E-1　open strings on the guitar

fret 1
fret 2
fret 3
fret 4

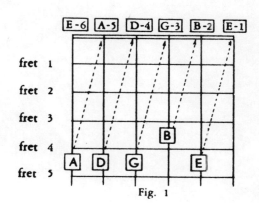

Fig. 1

LESSON 1

THE TOP THREE OPEN STRINGS

Right hand fingers will
be indicated as follows:

English	Spanish
1st. Index	= *Indice* = *(i)*
2nd. Middle	= *Medio* = *(m)*
3rd. Ring	= *Anular* = *(a)*
Thumb	= *Pulgar* = *(p)*

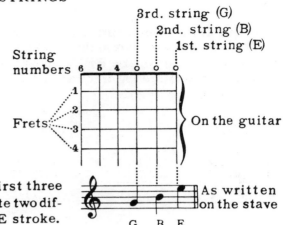

PREPARING THE RIGHT-HAND FINGERS

In vibrating the strings of the guitar the thumb *(p)* and first three fingers *(i-m-a)* of the right hand are called upon to execute two different types of stroke, i. e. the REST stroke and the FREE stroke.

PROCEDURE FOR THE REST STROKE: *(apoyando)*

(a) Tilt back of hand slightly to the LEFT. *(b)* Place the TIP of the finger on the string to be sounded. *(c)* Pull the finger across the string in a diagonal direction allowing it to come to rest against the next lower string.

PROCEDURE FOR THE FREE STROKE: *(tirando)*

Same procedure as for the rest stroke except that instead of allowing the finger to come to rest against the lower string it should move freely over the lower string. In either the REST or FREE stroke be sure to use the LEFT side of the finger-tips for the 1st. and 2nd fingers. The fingers should move as a complete unit being propelled from the knuckle joint. The direction and movement of the right-hand fingers are very important in the matter of tone production. If the REST stroke is used, the finger must NOT be allowed to straighten out but should maintain the curved position as in the FREE stroke. The hand should remain in the same position for either stroke. Your teacher will advise you as to which stroke to use first.

For the present, the tip of the THUMB *(p)* for hand support may rest against any of the three lower strings. The right arm, hand and fingers must be completely relaxed. The strings should be plucked across the lower half of the sound hole.

Repeat the following lines until you acquire a smooth even stroke with the TIPS of the fingers.

*Continue in the same manner.

LESSON 2
ALTERNATING FINGERING *(right hand)* ON THE FIRST THREE OPEN STRINGS

When using alternating fingering it is no longer necessary to place the finger on the string. Try having the finger away from the string and letting it stroke across the string coming to rest against the next lower string for the REST stroke, or moving freely over the lower string for the FREE stroke.

Repeat the following lines until you acquire a smooth even stroke with the tips of the fingers. Develop all three fingers equally.

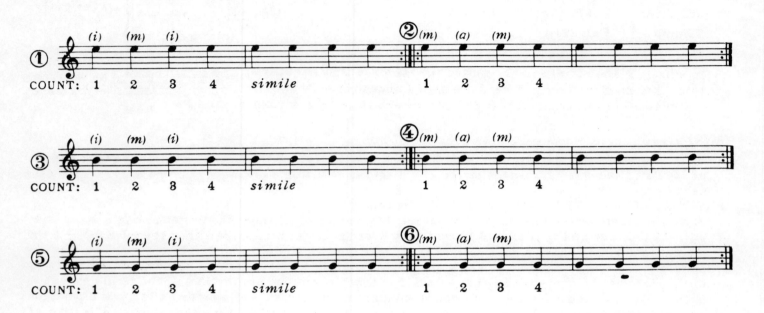

CHANGING STRINGS WITH ALTERNATING FINGERS

When alternating strings, the 1st. finger MUST reach BACK to the lower string and the 2nd. finger MUST reach AHEAD to the higher string. The same rule applies when using the 2nd. and 3rd. fingers, *i.e.* 2nd. finger *BACK*, 3rd. finger *AHEAD*.

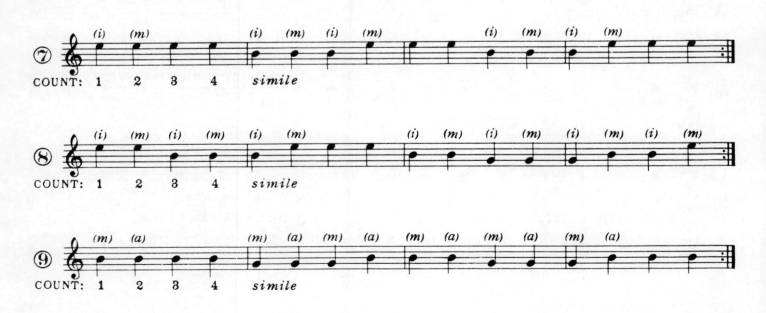

LESSON 3

THE THREE LOWER OPEN (bass) STRINGS

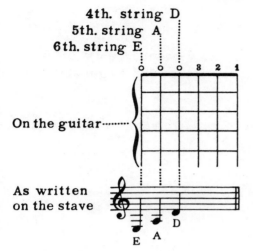

4th. string D
5th. string A
6th. string E

On the guitar

As written on the stave

E   A   D

PROCEDURE:

Use ONLY the right hand THUMB for the three lower bass strings.

For the present, to assist in holding the right hand steady while stroking the thumb, try resting the first three fingers upon the 8rd., 2nd. and 1st. strings.

Allow the thumb to stroke the string to be sounded and glide OVER the next higher string. It is most important when stroking the thumb that it be kept STRAIGHT across the string and come to rest 'outside' the first finger.

The string should be allowed to vibrate for the full value of the note.

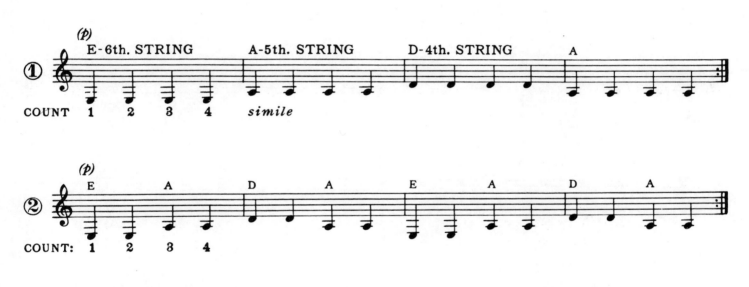

① (p)

E- 6th. STRING   A-5th. STRING   D- 4th. STRING   A

COUNT   1   2   3   4   *simile*

② (p)

E   A   D   A   E   A   D   A

COUNT: 1   2   3   4

③ (p)

E   A   D   A   E   A   D   A

COUNT: 1   2   3   4

④ (p)

COUNT: 1   2   3   4

4

LESSON 4
COMBINING BASS AND SOLO STRINGS

In the following studies use the THUMB *(p)* for the BASS strings. (Notes with stems pointing down are played with the thumb.) For the SOLO strings use the 1st. finger alone, then 2nd. finger alone, and then alternate 1st. and 2nd. fingers.

Also try alternating 2nd. and 3rd. fingers.

Learn to feel the position of the strings. Eyes on the music, not on the instrument. Practise diligently on this page to make the following pages easier.

Note these studies are two lines long.

LESSON 5

VARYING BOTH BASS AND SOLO OPEN STRINGS

In this lesson the 8rd. finger of the right hand is again brought into use. This lesson is most important for your future progress. CONSISTENTLY PRACTISE until you can play these examples smoothly without looking at your fingers.

*These are rests which will be explained later in the book.

LESSON 6

LEARNING NOTE VALUES

In order to play in correct time (rhythm) it is necessary to sustain some notes longer than others. To show the number of beats or counts that we hold a note, we have notes of different time values.

The symbol for counting is indicated at the beginning of the music as follows and is called the TIME SIGNATURE.

EXAMPLE: 4/4 equals four crotchets or the equivalent, (two minims), (one minim and two crotchets) or two crotchets and one minim in each bar.

COUNTING IN CROTCHETS AND MINIMS USING OPEN STRINGS ONLY

Be sure to maintain a smooth even rhythm while playing and counting. NO HESITATING. Play slowly at first, increasing the speed as you progress.

STUDY No. 1

STUDY No. 2

THE ELEMENTS OF MUSIC NOTATION

Music is represented on paper by a combination of characters and signs; it is necessary to learn all of these in order to play the Guitar intelligently.

Symbols called notes are written upon and between five lines 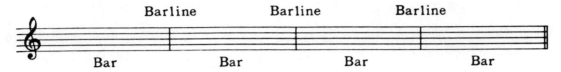 which is the stave.

The stave is divided by barlines into bars as follows:

These, in turn, are equal in time value, according to the fractional numbers, (Time signature) placed at the beginning of the music. The different time signatures will be introduced throughout the book as the need arises.

The Treble or G clef found at the beginning of the stave encircles the second line which establishes the note G on this line, from which the other lines and spaces are named as follows:

In addition notes are written upon and between short lines above and below the stave. These lines are called leger lines.

A rest indicates a pause, or silence for the value of the note after which it is named, such as

The end of a piece is indicated by a light and heavy line.

When a section or part of a piece is to be repeated it will be shown by a double bar with two dots.

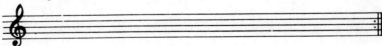

Key signatures, Sharps, Flats, and Naturals will be taken up and explained as the need arises.

LESSON 7

PREPARING THE LEFT-HAND FINGERS

The TIPS of the left-hand fingers should be pressed firmly upon the strings just BEHIND *(not on)* the frets. *(see illustration page V)* Be sure to keep the fingers close to the strings ready for action. NEVER LIFT A FINGER unless you have to: *i.e.* To sound the open string or to use it in another position.

The ball of the THUMB is placed against the underneath part of the neck approximately in line with the fret used by the second finger. *(see page V)*

LEARNING THE NOTES ON THE E, (1st) AND B, (2nd) STRINGS

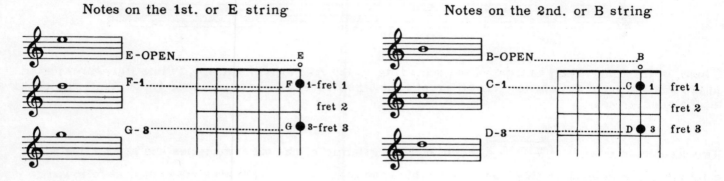

Notes on the 1st. or E string

Notes on the 2nd. or B string

PLUCKING THE STRINGS WITH THE RIGHT HAND FINGERS

Practise the following lines by first alternating with the 1st. and 2nd. fingers, and then with the 2nd. and 3rd. fingers.

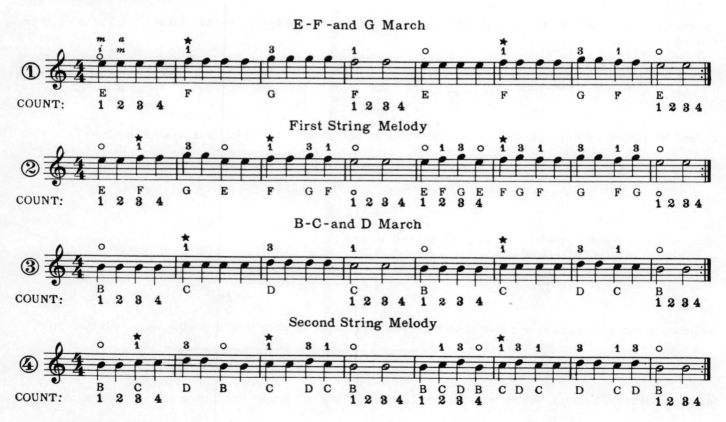

E-F-and G March

First String Melody

B-C-and D March

Second String Melody

*Hold fingers down

LESSON 8

NOTES ON THE G - 3rd STRING

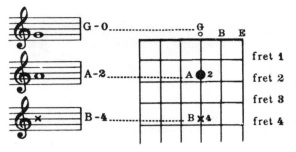

As you will observe there is but one fingered note (A) on this 3rd. string (G) before moving to the next higher (B) string.

To develop right hand finger action be sure to alternate 1st. and 2nd. fingers, then 2nd. and 3rd. fingers.

In order to avoid moving to the 2nd. string to sound the note B, (ex. 3-4-5) this note may be fingered on the G string with the 4th. finger (4th. fret) (see diagram)

Again use 1st. and 2nd. fingers, then 2nd. and 3rd. Be sure to count and observe note values as you play these studies.

TEST: How well do you know your fingering?

LESSON 9

SONGS TO PLAY USING THE THREE SOLO STRINGS

Work on these tunes until you can play them smoothly without looking at either hand for fingering or plucking. IMPORTANT: Play as indicated plucking with the 1st. and 2nd. fingers, then using the 2nd. and 3rd. fingers

MOUNTAIN TUNE

COUNT: 1 2 3 4

FOLK SONG

CHRISTMAS CAROL

COUNT: 1 2 3 4

FOLK SONG
Same song as No. 2 (different key)

AMERICAN TUNE

JUMPING JACK

LESSON 10

FINGERING NOTES ON THE THREE LOW BASS STRINGS

Draw thumb slightly under the neck, moving wrist outward to permit greater facility in finger action on these lower strings.

PROCEDURE: (*a*) Recite letter names of notes in strict rhythm.   (*b*) Recite fingering in rhythm. (*c*) Play and count without hesitating, play slowly at first.

Right hand thumb ONLY is used to pluck the bass strings. Press left-hand fingers firmly upon the strings just below (*not on*) the frets. Note that the fingers used for these notes are the same as the fret numbers.

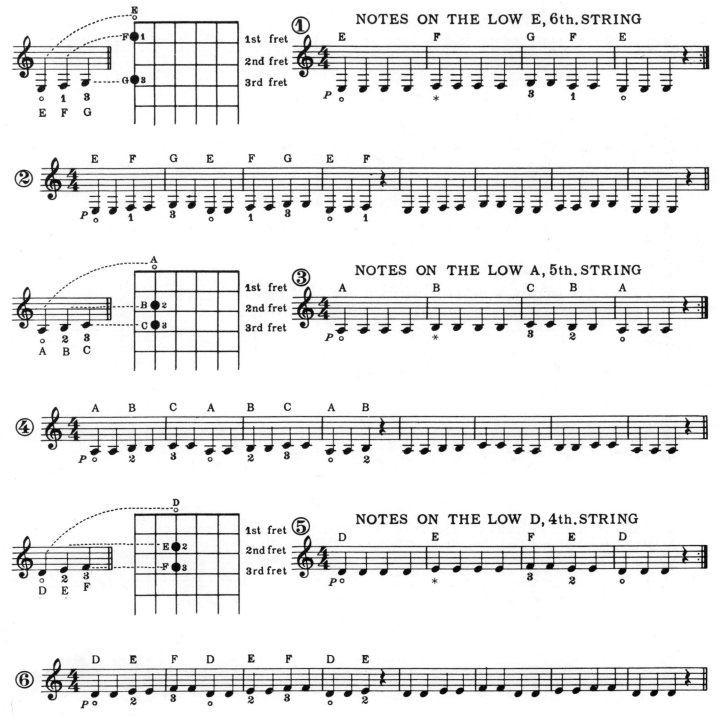

*Hold fingers down

LESSON 11

LEARNING A NEW RHYTHM AND TIME SIGNATURE

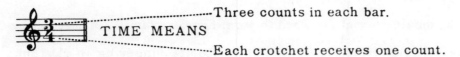

TIME MEANS ···· Three counts in each bar.

···· Each crotchet receives one count.

THE DOTTED MINIM

A DOTTED MINIM 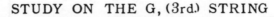 is equal in time value to three crotchets and makes a full bar in 3/4 time.

EXAMPLE : Two counts for the minim, one count for the dot (·). A DOT (·) is equal to one half the value of the note it follows.

STUDY ON THE G, (3rd.) STRING

Alternate 1st. and 2nd. fingers, right hand, then 2nd. and 3rd. fingers.

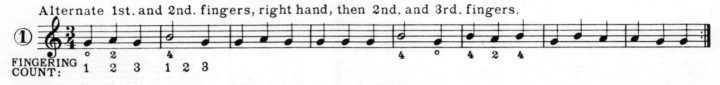

STUDY ON THE E, (1st.) STRING

Same as above.

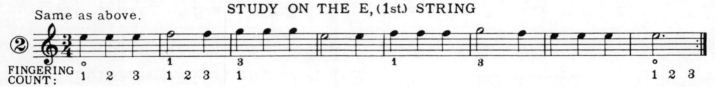

STUDY FOR THE THUMB ON THE BASS STRINGS

Recite letter names of notes before playing. Count while playing.

OLD FLEMISH MELODY

Many pieces begin with an incomplete bar and should be counted accordingly, Recite letter names. Count while playing. This melody starts on the 3rd. count.

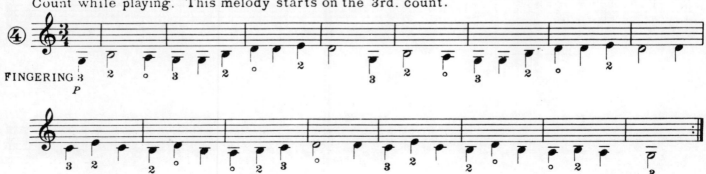

LESSON 12

SCALE CONSTRUCTION—DIATONIC MAJOR

A musical scale is a succession of notes from a given note to its octave, eight notes higher. The form or progression of all diatonic major scales is as follows:
Two whole tones, one semitone, three whole tones, one semitone. The semitones come between the 3rd. and 4th. and the 7th. and 8th. notes. The NATURAL half steps come between E & F and B & C (*see scale below*).

THE NATURAL OR C MAJOR SCALE

Not to be played

C MAJOR SCALE

Alternate 1st. and 2nd. fingers, (*right hand*) then 2nd. and 3rd. fingers. Use REST STROKE for all scale or scale passages. In ascending, hold left hand fingers down until changing to the next higher string.

Review of fingered notes (*left hand*) on all six strings. Name each note as you play and associate it with the finger used. Repeat until you do not have to think which finger to use.
HOLD LEFT-HAND FINGERS DOWN. RIGHT-HAND FINGERS, alternate 1st & 2nd then 2nd & 3rd

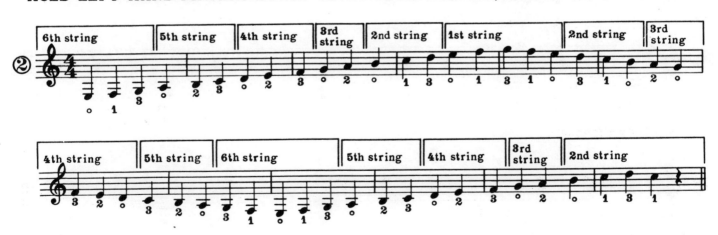

SHORT STUDY IN 3/4 TIME

Alternate right-hand fingering using 1st. & 2nd. then 2nd. & 3rd.

COUNT:

14

LESSON 13

PLAYING TWO OPEN STRINGS TOGETHER

Two notes written on the same stem are to be sounded together. Use (*right hand*) 1st. finger for the lower note, and 2nd. finger for the upper note. Also use the 2nd. finger for the lower note and the 3rd. finger for the upper note. The thumb may again be used to steady the hand. *REMEMBER!* RIGHT HAND RELAXED.

Adding open BASS strings (*right thumb*). Don't neglect the use of the 2nd. and 3rd. finger combination in all of these studies.

Note time signature

LESSON 14
PLAYING TWO NOTES TOGETHER

Plucking two strings (*right hand fingers*) while simultaneously using left-hand fingered notes. First pluck with 1st. and 2nd. fingers, then with 2nd. and 3rd. fingers, Develop all three fingers of the right hand equally.

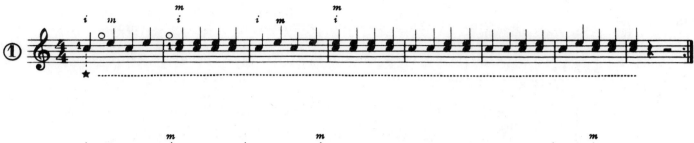

Remember! Hold fingers down whenever possible.

Note time signature

*Hold finger down

LESSON 15
CHANGING THE PITCH OF NOTES BY THE USE OF SHARPS
(*Learning new finger positions*)

A sharp (♯) placed in front of a note raises the pitch (sound) of that note by one semitone and requires a different fingering. To sharpen a note use the next higher fret. From one fret to the next, either up or down the fingerboard, is a semitone or half-step. To play a whole tone (*two semitones*) you must SKIP one fret. For one-and-a-half tones you SKIP TWO frets.

INTRODUCING G SHARP (G♯) 3rd string, and the A MINOR (*harmonic*) SCALE

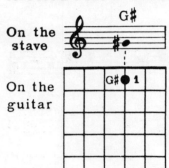

On the stave

On the guitar

The difference between the major (*Lesson 12*) and minor scales is the position of the tones and semitones. In the harmonic minor scale the semitones come between the 2nd & 3rd, 5th & 6th and 7th & 8th tones, with a tone and one-half between the 6th & 7th notes.

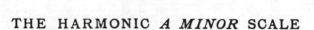

Ascending   Descending

THE HARMONIC *A MINOR* SCALE

Alternate 1st & 2nd fingers (*right hand*) then 2nd & 3rd fingers.
Use the REST STROKE in all scale passages.

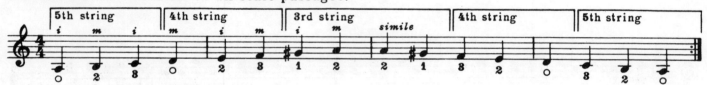

LEARNING THE VALUE OF QUAVERS

This ♪ is a quaver which is equal to one half the value of a crotchet.

When written in groups of two or more they are connected by a line: ♫ or ♬
A quaver rest (𝄾) receives the same count as a quaver.

A NEW TIME SIGNATURE   2 ⸻ two counts in each bar.
                equals
             4 ⸻ a crotchet receives one count.

COUNTING QUAVERS

COUNT: 1 & 2 & 1 & 2 & 1 & 2 & 1 & 2 & 1 & 2 &

STUDY No. 1
Using thumb and three fingers of the right hand, Count evenly.

COUNT: 1 & 2 & 1 & 2 & 1 & 2 & *simile*

STUDY No. 2
Recite letter names of notes before playing. Keep a steady rhythm.

COUNT: 1 & 2 & 1 & 2 & 1 & 2 & *simile*

INTRODUCING: SEMIBREVE — ACCIDENTALS

This  is a semibreve and receives 4 counts or taps. This means that the tone (*sound*) of a semibreve must be maintained for the full count of the bar in ⁴⁄₄ time. Be sure to count and maintain an even, steady rhythm. Play slowly at first.

An accidental is a sharp (♯) or flat (♭) which is not in the key signature and applies ONLY to the rest of the bar in which it first appears. In the examples below a sharp is applied to every G, raising each a semitone to G♯.

STUDY No. 1

Be sure to allow the open bass strings to vibrate for their full value.

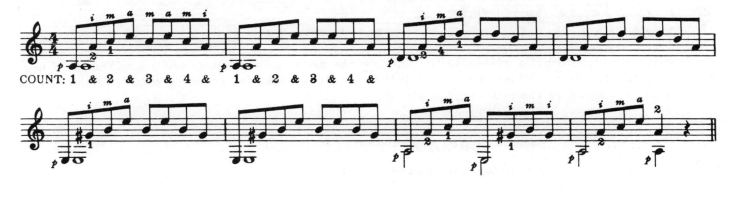

COUNT: 1 & 2 & 3 & 4 & 1 & 2 & 3 & 4 &

STUDY No. 2

COUNT: 1 & 2 & 3 4 1 & 2 & 3 4

1 & 2 3 & 4

STUDY No. 3

Note time signature.

COUNT: 1 2 3 1 2 3

STUDY No. 4

Note change in time signature.

COUNT: 1 & 2 1 & 2

CHROMATIC AND ENHARMONIC NOTATION

The word "CHROMATIC" means moving by semitones or half-steps.   A CHROMATIC scale is one that ascends or descends by semitones.

ENHARMONIC notes *sound the same* even though they are notated (*written*) on different lines or spaces of the stave and are called by different names, such as (F♯ *or* G♭, C♯ *or* D♭), etc.

A Sharp (♯) RAISES the pitch of the note to which it applies by one semitone or fret.

A Flat (♭) LOWERS the pitch of a note by one semitone or fret.

A Natural sign (♮) restores the note to its original pitch.

EXAMPLE: (*not to be played*).   The ENHARMONIC NOTES are bracketed.   STUDY them.

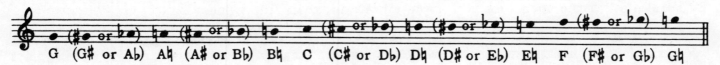

G   (G♯ or A♭)   A♮   (A♯ or B♭)   B♮   C   (C♯ or D♭)   D♮   (D♯ or E♭)   E♮   F   (F♯ or G♭)   G♮

Practise these chromatic scales daily, naming the notes as you finger and sound them.   Chromatic scales provide excellent use of the left-hand 4th finger. In ascending, hold left-hand fingers down until changing to the next higher string.

CHROMATIC SCALE IN G

Ascending using sharps, descending using flats

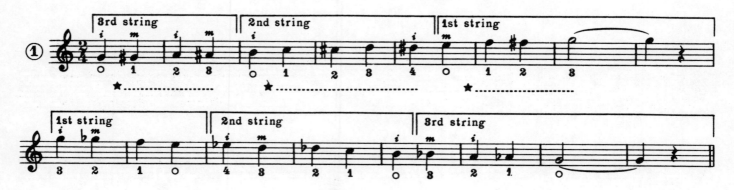

CHROMATIC SCALE USING BASS STRINGS

Ascending using sharps, descending using flats

*Hold fingers down

LESSON 18

*ANDANTE IN C MAJOR

Ferdinando Carulli

Bass notes must be held down by the left-hand fingers for their full **value**.

*Andante—In a moderate tempo but flowing gracefully.

INTRODUCING TWO F SHARPS (*F♯*) AND TWO C SHARPS (*C♯*) (*See diagrams*)

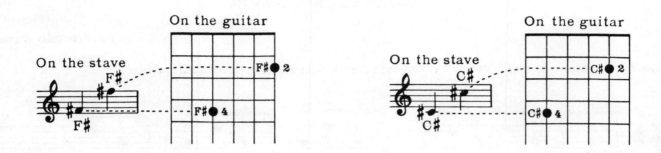

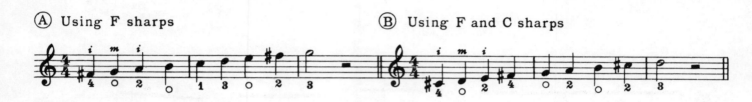

STUDY IN C MAJOR
(using F and C sharps)

F. Carulli

LEARNING THE SCALE AND KEY OF G MAJOR
One sharp — F♯

Notice the key signature and remember to sharpen each F.

LEARNING THE SCALE AND KEY OF E MINOR
The key of E minor has the same key signature as G major

WALTZ

Remember to sharpen each F

F. Carulli

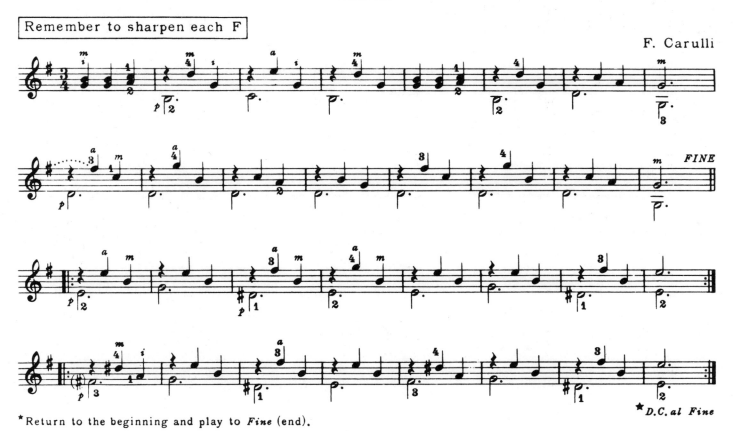

*Return to the beginning and play to *Fine* (end).

LESSON 21

ALLEGRO MODERATO★

Mauro Giuliani

To review using G♯. *See Lesson 15.*
Practise slowly at first, gradually increasing the speed.

★ Allegro moderato— Moderately fast

LESSON 22

FURTHER LEFT-HAND FINGER DEVELOPMENT

To facilitate the execution, and further development, of the left hand fingers, it is recommended to practise the following C Major Scale without using open strings. Do this from memory and play several times at each practice period, carefully observing the new fingering.

Learn to sufficiently separate the fingers without moving the hand. In ascending scales, it is advisable to hold the fingers down after a note has been sounded and then take them all off when you move to the next higher string. This is rather difficult for the beginner but is essential to smooth legato playing. This technique is normal in ascending scale passages.

REMEMBER: Never lift a finger until you have to.

C MAJOR SCALE
No open strings

PLAYING THREE-NOTE CHORDS

PROCEDURE: First play notes of chord separately, then stroke all three notes simultaneously. Be sure to hold fingers down whenever possible. Special attention should be given to the 3rd. finger (*a*).

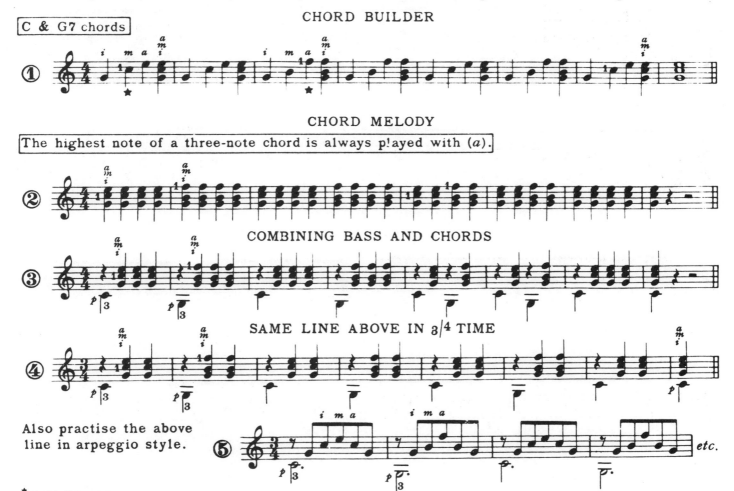

Also practise the above line in arpeggio style.

*Hold finger down

LESSON 23

A study in wide string crossings for the right hand fingers.

WALTZ IN C MAJOR

F. Carulli

In moderate waltz tempo

Printed in England by Commercial Colour Press, 9/93 (16109)

26

LESSON 24

FURTHER THREE-NOTE CHORDS

CHORD BUILDER

A minor & E major chords

CHORDAL MELODY

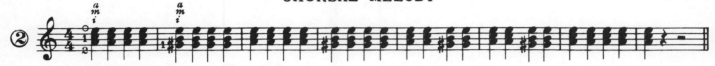

COMBINING BASS AND CHORDS

Also practise the above line in arpeggio style.

MELODY IN BASS WITH CHORD ACCOMPANIMENT ★★

C. P. H.

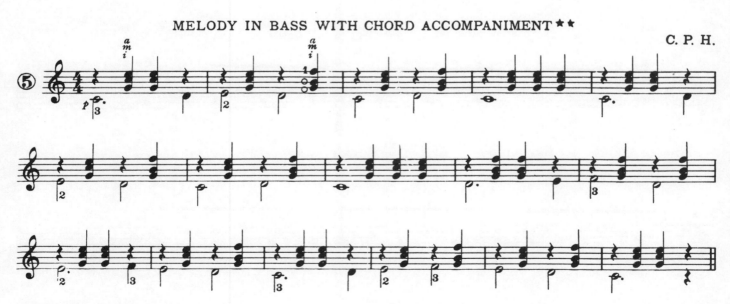

★ Hold fingers down

★★ Maintain a smooth melody line in the bass.